SHORT CIRCULAR WALKS IN THE PEAK DISTRICT
BY
JOHN N. MERRILL

Maps and Photographs by John N. Merrill

a J.N.M. PUBLICATION

1986

D1262630

a J.N.M. PUBLICATION

J.N.M. PUBLICATIONS,
WINSTER,
MATLOCK,
DERBYSHIRE,
DE4 2DQ.

This book is copyright under the Berne Convention. All rights are reserved. Apart from any fair dealing for the purposes of private study, research, criticism or review, as permitted under the Copyright Act, 1956, no part of this publication may be reproduced, stored in a retrieval system, or transmitted in any other form by any means, electronic, electrical, chemical, mechanical, optical, photocopying, recording or otherwise, without the prior permission of the copyright owner. Enquiries should be addressed to the publishers.

Conceived, edited, typeset and designed by John N. Merrill.

© Text and Routes— John N. Merrill 1986

© Maps and photographs—John N. Merrill 1986

First published 1983.

Reprinted twice 1984.

This revised edition March 1986.

ISBN 0 907496 37 7

Typesetting interfaced by:
Steve Rothwell Typesetting Services, 20 St Ann's Square, Manchester M2 7HG.

Printed by: Higham Press Ltd., New Street, Shirland, Derbyshire.

J.N.M. Publications, Winster, Derbyshire, DE4 2DQ.

John Merrill.

ABOUT JOHN N. MERRILL

John combines the characteristics and strength of a mountain climber with the stamina, and athletic capabilities of a marathon runner. In this respect he is unique and has to his credit a whole string of remarkable long walks. He is without question the world's leading marathon walker.

Over the last ten years he has walked more than 55,000 miles and successfully completed ten walks of at least 1,000 miles or more.

His six walks in Britain are—

Hebridean Journey ....1,003 miles
Northern Isles Journey...913 miles
Irish Island Journey..1,578 miles
Parkland Journey..2,043 miles
Lands End to John O'Groats ....1,608 miles

and in 1978 he became the first person (permanent Guinness Book Of Records entry) to walk the entire coastline of Britain—6,824 miles in ten months.

In Europe he has walked across Austria (712 miles), hiked the Tour of Mont Blanc and GR20 in Corsica as training! In 1982 he walked across Europe—2,806 miles in 107 days—crossing seven countries, the Swiss and French Alps and the complete Pyrennean chain—the hardest and longest mountain walk in Europe.

In America he used the world's longest footpath—The Appalachian Trail (2,200 miles) as a training walk. The following year he walked from Mexico to Canada in record time—118 days for 2,700 miles.

During the summer of 1984, John set off from Virginia Beach on the Atlantic coast, and walked 4,226 miles without a rest day, across the width of America to San Francisco and the Pacific Ocean. This walk is unquestionably his greatest achievement, being, in modern history, the longest, hardest crossing of the USA in the shortest time—under six months (177 days). The direct distance is 2,800 miles.

Between major walks John is out training in his own area —the Peak District National Park. As well as walking in other areas of Britain and in Europe he has been trekking in the Himalayas four times. He lectures extensively and is author of more than sixty books.

CONTENTS

INTRODUCTION 1

EDALE—RUSHUP EDGE—6 Miles 3

HOPE—WIN HILL—4 Miles 5

STANAGE EDGE—ALONG A GRITSTONE EDGE—3 Miles 7

HATHERSAGE—A HISTORICAL WALK 4 Miles 9

BASLOW—EDGES WALK—5 Miles 11

BAKEWELL TOWN WALK—1½ Miles 13

BAKEWELL—WYE VALLEY AND HADDON HALL—4 Miles 15

BEELEY—WOOD AND MOOR—3 Miles 17

ALPORT—LATHKILL DALE AND YOULGREAVE—3 Miles 19

TIDESWELL—TWO DALES AND FOUR INNS—4½ Miles 21

LONGNOR—DOVE AND MANIFOLD VALLEY—3 Miles 23

HARTINGTON—UPPER DOVE VALLEY—5 Miles 25

TISSINGTON—PEAK DISTRICT'S PRETTIEST VILLAGE—3 Miles .. 27

BRASSINGTON—LIMESTONE AND HIGH PEAK TRAIL—5 Miles 29

ILAM AND BLORE PASTURES—4 Miles 31

OTHER BOOKS BY JOHN MERRILL— 33

WALK RECORD CHART— 36

RIVER WYE—BAKEWELL

INTRODUCTION

With more than 9,000 public rights of way in Derbyshire, totaling more than 3,000 miles, there is endless scope to explore the county on foot. The Peak District is an extraordinarily rich area of countryside, containing a remarkable diversity of scenery and history. My aim has been to select fifteen walks of between 3 and 6 miles long, which together illustrates the variety of walking to be found in the area.

All the walks are new ones, and stem from the requests for more short walks by the many who have walked my earlier short walk guides. Each walk starts from a car park and follows rights of way around a particular scenic area. Some of the paths are little used, but I hope this encourages their use for they do bring you to good vantage points. All the walks include somewhere for refreshments, and in the main there is a local pub; helping to make the two-hour outing a more enjoyable stroll in the countryside. One walk does have four pubs, and it is possible to visit all during opening hours!

I have endeavoured to be as accurate as possible with the walking instructions and maps, but it is useful to carry the appropriate Ordnance Survey map with you. I do hope these walks will give you endless pleasure, and that you will follow in my footsteps around, through, and over some of the finest walking terrain in Britain.

Happy walking,

John N. Merrill.

JOHN N. MERRILL
WINSTER

ILAM HALL—YOUTH HOSTEL AND
NATIONAL TRUST INFORMATION CENTRE

1

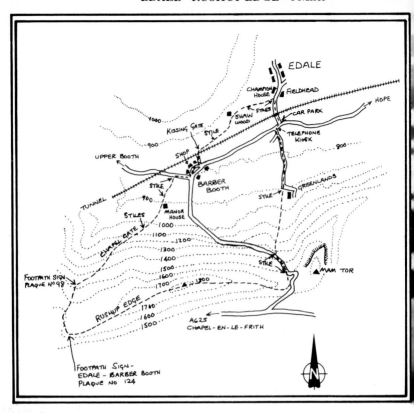

EDALE CROSS

EDALE—RUSHUP EDGE—
6 miles—*allow 3 hours*

MAPS—O.S. 1:25,000 Outdoor Leisure Map—The Dark Peak. O.S. 1:50,000 Sheet No. 110 - Sheffield and Huddersfield.

CAR PARK—Edale, at junction of village road.

ABOUT THE WALK—Edale, the start of the Pennine Way, is in the midst of some of the finest high level walking in the Peak District. This walk takes you onto Rushup Edge, providing distant views to Edale and its valley. Much of the time you are following old packhorse routes.

WALKING INSTRUCTIONS—Turn right outside the car park entrance and pass a telephone kiosk on your left. Shortly afterwards turn left along a track, signposted—Bridlepath—Castleton 1¾ miles'. Keep to the left-hand track as you ascend gently past a farm on your right. Beyond you enter Harden Clough. Where the track turns sharp left, keep straight ahead on well—used stiled path. The path keeps close to a small stream on your left as you begin ascending more steeply. ½ mile from the track you gain the minor road, via a stile. Turn left, and after 150 yards leave the road via a stile on your right and follow the distinct footpath. On your left rises the steep slopes of Mam Tor. 150 yards later, on approaching the road, bear right and follow the signposted path first above the road before ascending onto Rushup Edge. Here, at last the principal ascending is over.

Rushup Edge, National Trust property, is a magnificent vantage point, and for the next 1½ miles you keep to the wide path along its ridge. In ¾ mile you reach the highest point —1,800 feet. Continue ahead on the path, crossing the stiles as you bear slightly left away from the crest of the now broad ridge, as you gently descend. ¼ mile later you reach the footpath sign for Edale/Barber Booth. The sign was erected by the Peak District Northern Counties Footpath Preservation Society and is plaque No. 124. Turn right on a distinct path. ¼ mile later, bear right on the path and begin descending down Chapel Gate, crossing a footpath to Brown Knoll. At the bottom of the steep descent, cross two stiles and begin crossing the fields to the lefthand side of Manor House. The whole path is well-stiled. Past the house the path bears right and descends to the road close to Barber Booth. Turn right, and at the road junction moments later left, past the village shop. Just beyond the bend turn left, as footpath-signed, and follow the track over the railway line. On the other side of the bridge turn right, through a kissing gate, and follow the well-stiled path across the fields to the right of Shaw Wood Farm. Bear right here through the stiles and continue across the fields to Edale, reaching the road at Champion House. To your left is Fieldhead, the National Park Information Centre. Turn right along the road past the aptly-named Rambler Inn to reach the car park.

PACKHORSE ROUTES—Edale was a principal centre for packhorse teams, with five separate routes radiating out. One via Barber Booth and on to Edale Cross; another via Chapel Gate; Mam Tor and Winnats; to Castleton via Hollins Cross; and the final one via Nether Booth to Hope Cross. The word 'Booth', which was recorded in the 15th Century onwards, means a place where shepherds and herdsmen sheltered.

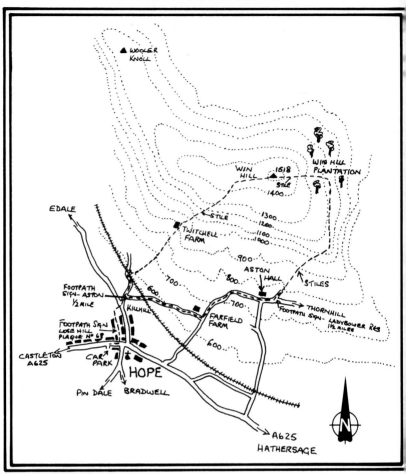

HOPE CHURCH

4

HOPE—WIN HILL—4 Miles—*allow 2½ hours*

MAPS—O.S. 1:25,000 Outdoor Leisure Map—The Dark Peak. O.S. 1:50,000 Sheet 110—Sheffield and Huddersfield.

CAR PARK—In centre of Hope village on lefthand side of A625 road.

ABOUT THE WALK—A short ascent of the Peak District's loftiest mountain. The view from its summit over the surrounding area is extensive.

WALKING INSTRUCTIONS—From the car park entrance turn right and left almost immediately past the Blacksmith's Cottage onto the footpath-signed path—Lose Hill. Plaque No. 68. The path, which is well-stiled, passes between the houses, across a small housing estate. At the end of the next field turn right through two stiles and descend the field to the road at Killhill. On your right is a large white house. Cross the Edale road and descend the minor road. Cross the river Noe, and just past the house on your right, turn right as signposted for 'Aston' ½ mile. The path is a wide track, tarmaced at first, with a cemetery on your left. The track passes under the Manchester railway line before curving right to the minor road just past Farfield Farm. Turn left and follow the lane through Aston village. Continue on the road past Aston Hall on your left, ignoring the road on your right. A little past the hall turn left, as footpath-signposted - 'Ladybower Reservoir' 1½ miles. The path is defined and well-stiled as you begin ascending the fields, passing a narrow plantation on your left. At the top of the field you ascend a ladder stile. Bear slightly right, but ascending on the footpath signposted 'Win Hill'. Shortly afterwards the path levels out as you contour round the eastern slopes of Win Hill. Eventually you join a wide path with a gritstone wall on your left. Follow this to Win Hill Plantation, where you turn left and ascend for the last time to the rocky summit of Win Hill, ascending a ladder stile en route.

Descend the gritstone ridge of Win Hill, and at the third mound of stones turn left along the wide path and begin the gradual, then steep, descent to the ruins of Twitchell Farm. At the top of the steep section you reach a crossroads of paths. Keep straight ahead—'Hope' ¾ mile. From the farm you descend a track, which after ¼ mile bears right and passes under the Manchester railway. Here turn left and descend the now tarmaced lane back to Killhill and your starting-out path. Retrace your steps back into Hope.

WIN HILL—1,518 feet—A spectacular viewpoint with a small gritstone summit ridge. According to legend, this hill and the other opposite—Lose Hill—was the scene of a battle in the 7th Century. The opposing armies occupied the hills. The next day the armies descended and the battle raged in the valley below. At the end of the day the battle was over. The winners' hill where they camped became known as Win Hill, and the losers'—Lose Hill.

HOPE CHURCH—Dedicated to St. Peter and dates from the early 15th Century. Inside are grave slabs, Jacobean pews, and a coat of arms to the Eyre family who were the principal landowners in the area. The schoolmaster's chair has a latin inscription meaning—'You cannot make a scholar out of a block of wood'.

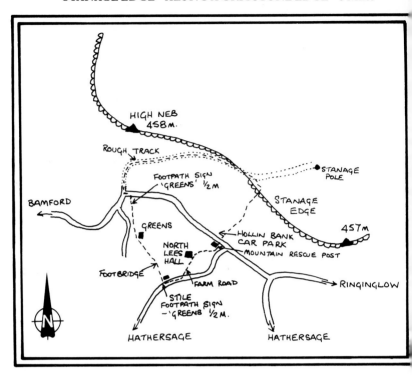

GRITSTONE EDGE AND MILLSTONES

STANAGE EDGE—along a gritstone edge—
3 miles—*allow 1½ hours*

MAPS—O.S. 1:50,000 Sheet 110—Sheffield and Huddersfield. - O.S. 1:25,000 Sheet SK 28/38—Sheffield

CAR PARK - Hollin Bank beneath Stanage Edge at Grid Ref. SK238838.

ABOUT THE WALK—Stanage Edge is the longest edge in the Peak District. It provides a good vantage point for walkers, and for climbers there are 600 routes of varying difficulty. The walk combines a visit to the Edge with a walk through woodland and past an extraordinarily fine Elizabeth building—North Lees Hall.

WALKING INSTRUCTIONS—From the car park entrance turn left, and at the Mountain Rescue post, shortly afterwards on your right, turn right and descend the path for Hathersage on the immediate left of the building. At the track below, turn right and begin descending to North Lees Hall, now owned by Peak Park Planning Board. At the buildings bear left, and continue descending the now tarmaced track past the Hall on your right. At the road ¼ mile later turn right, and after 200 yards turn right and follow the signposted path to Greens House, ½ mile away. First you cross a field before entering woodland and a small stream. Cross the stream via the wooden footbridge and ascend the well—defined path to Greens House. Continue ascending past the house, first to your right then to your left to the right-hand side of a plantation. At the road beside the plantation is a footpath sign for Greens House.

Turn left along the road, and, where it turns sharp left around the other side of the plantation, turn right and leave the road for a track which begins curving right and ascend onto Stanage Edge, a mile away. On gaining the Edge leave the track and follow the path along the top of the Edge, on your right. After a short distance along here you reach the path which descends down to the car park. Turn right and descend the well-used path.

NORTH LEES HALL—The Eyre family were principal land owners in the Hope Valley during the 15th, 16th and 17th Centuries. In the 16th Century they had several Halls in the area, including North Lees. The exact date when this very fine Elizabethan tower house was built is not known. The Hall was built by William Jessop of Broom Hall, Sheffield, and the plasterwork bears the date 1594. The Eyres were devout Roman Catholics, and in 1685 a chapel was built beneath the hall. During the Glorious Revolution of 1688 it was ransacked and demolished. As you cross the field to Greens House you can see a solitary arched window on your right; this is all that remains of the chapel. Charlotte Bronte's novel, 'Jane Eyre', has many places identifiable with the area, and North Lees Hall is said to be Thornfield.

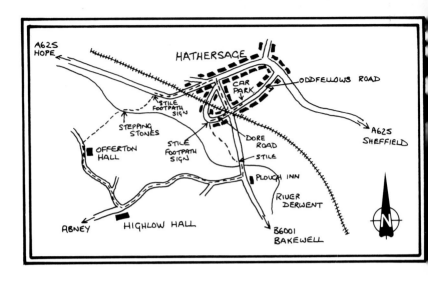

DERWENT STEPPING STONES NR. HATHERSAGE

HATHERSAGE—a historical walk—
4 miles—allow 2 hours

MAPS—O.S. 1:50,000 Sheet 110—Sheffield and Huddersfield. - O.S. 1:25,000 Sheet SK 28/38—Sheffield

CAR PARK—Central Hathersage on Oddfellows Road.

ABOUT THE WALK—Hathersage has an interesting past, with needle factories, an impressive church, Little John's grave, and many fine old Halls in its vicinity. This walk takes you into the surrounding area to see two extremely fine buildings, before returning you to the village via the River Derwent.

WALKING INSTRUCTIONS—Turn right out of the car park along Oddfellows Road. Turn left onto B6001 Grindleford Road, and 100 yards later turn right and descend Dore Lane and walk under the railway. Where the road turns right at the entrance to Nether Hall, turn left, and follow the footpath as signposted, across the fields to the road (B6001), bridge and River Derwent. Turn right and cross the road bridge, and opposite the Plough Inn, on your left, turn right and ascend Abney road. For the next mile to Highlow Hall you follow this minor road.

At the Hall turn right and follow the track to Offerton Hall, left at the track junction after the first ¼ mile. Just past Offerton Hall, turn right as footpath-signposted, and descend the fields to the River Derwent. Turn right and left almost immediately, and cross the river via the curving stepping stones. On the other side turn right and follow the path, first close to the river before ascending to the main road (A625). Turn right and walk into Hathersage. Opposite the George Hotel, turn right, and 300 yards up here turn left into Oddfellows Road and car park.

HATHERSAGE HALLS—In the 16th Century Robert Eyre, the principal landowner of the Hope Valley with more than 22,000 acres, had seven sons. For each of them he built a Hall, within sight of each other. Robert Eyre lived at Highlow Hall, and it is said that by raising a flag he could summon one or all of his seven sons. The Halls he built were Moorseats, Shatton, Nether Shatton, Hazleford, Offerton, Crookhill and North Lees.

HIGHLOW HALL—16th Century with impressive Jacobean gateway. A ghost story still lingers about the Hall concerning the Eyres. The Hall passed by marriage into the Eyre family when Nicholas Eyre married the younger of two sisters of the Archers family. It is said that Nicholas was at first betrothed to the older sister, but soon turned his affection to the younger. In time they married, and the older fled after cursing the Eyres on the great staircase. It is said that the Eyres lost their property within the prophesied time.

OFFERTON HALL—A large memorial house dating back to about 1558 with considerable rebuilding and enlarging in 1658.

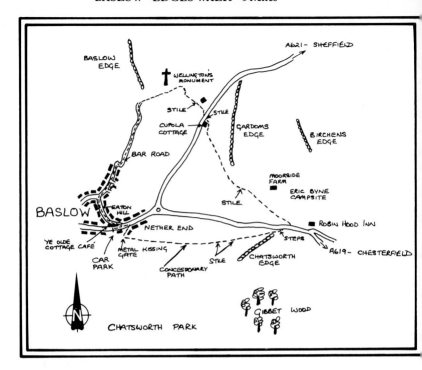

EAGLE STONE —BASLOW EDGE

ROBIN HOOD INN

GRITSTONE EDGES—Derbyshire has numerous Edges, with faces up to 120 feet high. Since the 1950s they have become popular climbing grounds, and during the summer months and weekends dozens of climbers can be seen scaling the different graded routes.

BASLOW—EDGES WALK—
5 miles—*allow 2½ hours*

MAPS—O.S. 1:25,000 Outdoor Leisure Map—The White Peak (East Sheet)
O.S. 1:50,000 Sheet 119—Buxton, Matlock and Dove Dale.

CAR PARK—Nether End, Baslow.

ABOUT THE WALK—A steady ascent from Baslow brings you to a vantage point overlooking the Derwent Valley to Chatsworth Park, through which you walk later. This walk through gritstone scenery takes you close to four Edges and through woodland. A pub two-thirds of the way fortifies you for the final 1½ miles.

WALKING INSTRUCTIONS—From the car park cross the grass triangle and walk up Eaton Hill road on the immediate right of Ye Olde Cottage Cafe. At the top of the road turn right and follow Bar Road (No Through Road) as it ascends past the houses and deteriorates to a track. Continue on the walled track for the next ½ mile. Where you leave the walled track behind and enter open country, turn right along the path close to a wall on your right and beneath Wellington's monument. Where you turned right, on your left can be seen Baslow Edge. Continue on the well-used path in woodland before turning sharp right and descending to the Sheffield A621 road, en route passing a house on your left, two stiles and a bridge. Turn left at the road, and right almost immediately over the stile on the left of Cupola Cottage. You are now on the well-defined path beneath Gardoms Edge. Bear right and follow the path as it angles up gently across the walled and grass slope. After a little over ¼ mile you bear left and walk through a sparse wood to the top and stile. Just beyond the path divides; keep to the right hand one. The left path goes to Moorside Farm and the Eric Byne Campsite. On your left is Birchens Edge. Cross the bracken—covered terrain and descend to the road (A619), stile and footpath sign. Almost opposite is the concessionary path through Chatsworth Park, and on your left is the Robin Hood's Inn.

Descend the steps of the concessionary path before crossing a footbridge. Bear right and ascend to a track. Follow this to your right, passing Chatsworth Edge on your left. ½ mile along this track brings you to two very high stiles before entering Chatsworth Park. Here you keep straight ahead, following the signposted path to Baslow—1 mile. Yellow arrows on trees indicate the route. A little over ½ mile you reach the main Baslow path at a large iron kissing gate. Turn right through the gate and follow the track to Bar End and back into Nether End.

GIBBETTING—As you walk through Chatsworth Park on your left is a wood known as Gibbet Wood and a moorland beyond known as Gibbet Moor. Reaching Bar End, you passed a thatched cottage on your right. All are linked to a macabre event more than 200 years ago. Gibbetting in the 18th Century was a popular form of punishment. On this occasion a tramp had finally obtained food by force from the cook at the cottage. He was so incensed that she would not let him have any, that in his rage he picked up a pan of hot fat and poured it down her throat, killing her. He was caught three days later, and for his crime was sentenced to be gibbeted alive. He was suspended in a metal frame at the scene of the crime. At night his screams could be heard for miles, and the Duke of Devonshire resolved that this would be the last live gibbet in Derbyshire.

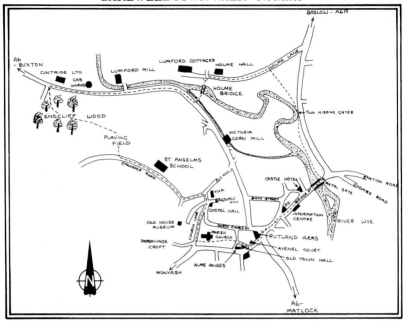

HISTORY NOTES—in walking order—

RUTLAND ARMS HOTEL—built in 1804. The cook here in 1859 misunderstood her instructions and made by mistake the now famous 'Bakewell Pudding'. Jane Austen stayed here in 1811, and parts of the area can be identified in her novel—'Pride and Prejudice'.

OLD MARKET HALL—now Information Centre. Built in the 17th Century.

WYE BRIDGE—one of the oldest in the country. Five pointed arches and built about 1300.

HOLME HALL—Tudor building with terraced walled garden, built in 1626.

LUMSFORD MILL—former cotton spinning mill, which in 1778 employed 300 people. The mill was driven by two waterwheels, the largest being 25 feet in diameter.

OLD HOUSE MUSEUM—a former yeoman house with wattle and daub walls dating back to 1534. Now a local museum.

PARISH CHURCH—dates from Norman times with doorway. The south porch has fragments of both Saxon and Norman workmanship, and the churchyard has two Saxon cross shafts. The octagonal tower and spire were built in 1340. The Vernon Chapel was built twenty years later and houses a large tomb to Sir John Manners and Dorothy Vernon, whose elopement is one of Derbyshire's most romantic legends. Opposite is a tomb to Sir George Manners and a table tomb to Sir George Vernon known as the King of the Peak.

OLD TOWN HALL—17th Century. Built in 1602 and was formerly the town hall and courtroom. This century the fire engine was stored here, and in 1964 it was a chip shop! Just above the town hall are six almshouses built in 1709.

AVENEL COURT—mediaeval building.

BAKEWELL TOWN WALK—
1½ miles—*allow 1 hour*

CAR PARKS—several in Bakewell—behind the Information Office, opposite Library, off Water Lane, and off Coombs Road.

ABOUT THE WALK—Bakewell, the administrative capital of the Peak District, is full of history and has many exceptional buildings. This short walk takes you to many of the town's features while sampling its location beside the River Wye and views of the Wye valley.

WALKING INSTRUCTIONS—From Rutland Square walk down the road past the Post Office on your left and the Information Centre on your right; now on Bridge Street. After crossing the River Wye, turn left through the metal gate and walk close to the River Wye. First to two kissing gates and then across the field to Holme Lane. Turn left along the road, with Holme Hall on you right. Just before Lumsford Cottages, turn left and cross the River Wye via the Holme Bridge. At the Buxton Road (A6), turn right. Pass Lumsford Mill on your right, then the Gas Works, and just past Cintride Ltd. turn left onto a factory drive. Turn left immediately and follow the well-worn ascending path through Endcliff Wood. The path bears left to St. Anselm's playing fields, which you cross to footpath sign and Stanedge Road.

Turn left, passing the school on your left as you descend. At Fly Hill turn right and right again shortly afterwards to walk along Church Lane. Off this is the signposted path to the Old House Museum. At the entrance to Parsonage Croft, turn left and walk through the churchyard, passing the church on your left. Beyond the church bear right through the rest of the graveyard.At Church Alley, turn left then right immediately to pass the Old Town Hall and onto King Street. Descend this to Rutland Square and the Rutland Arms. To complete your appreciation of Bakewell, why not visit the Original Pudding Shop and sample one of those mouth-watering puddings?

HOLME BRIDGE—packhorse bridge, with low parapets, built in 1626.

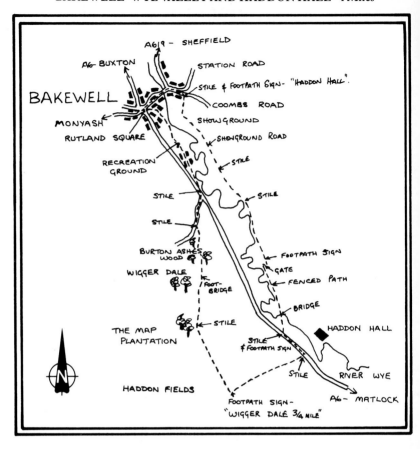

HADDON HALL—UPPER TERRACE

BAKEWELL—WYE VALLEY & HADDON HALL—4 miles—*allow 2 hours*

MAPS—O.S. 1:25,000 Outdoor Leisure Map—The White Peak (East Sheet)
O.S. 1:50,000 Sheet 119—Buxton, Matlock and Dove Dale.

CAR PARK—Central Bakewell.

ABOUT THE WALK—Leaving Bakewell, this short walk on its southern side takes you along the valley floor beside the River Wye to the historic Haddon Hall. To return to Bakewell, the route ascends the valley side to obtain views of the Hall and valley before descending through woodland back into central Bakewell.

WALKING INSTRUCTIONS—From Rutland Square walk along the main street past the Information Centre and cross the River Wye. Turn right along Coombs Road, and 150 yards later turn right, as footpath-signposted for Haddon Hall. At the end of the fenced path turn left along the showground road. After ¼ mile continue ahead with the hedge on your left along the path to the banks of the River Wye. Keep to the bank side for ¼ mile before ascending above a wide loop of the river to a track. Turn right and left immediately along a fenced path, which after ¼ mile crosses the River Wye via a substantial footpath bridge.

At the A6 road turn left, and 300 yards later at the entrance to Haddon Hall turn right, and follow the walled track signposted for Youlgreave. Nearing the end of the second field, with good views to Haddon Hall, turn right as signposted for Wigger Dale ¾ mile. At first the path is undefined across the large field. Aim for The Map Plantation, and you will reach the stile. Bear slightly right, and opposite the plantation is the stile and descending path; almost due north, to Wigger Dale. Go round the right-hand edge of a small wood and cross a stream via a footbridge. Ascend the field beyond to the stile and wide path through Burton Ashes Wood. On the other side of the wood keep the hedge on your immediate right and gain the stile on the left of the gate. Turn right and descend the farm road to the A6.

Almost opposite on your right is the stile and path. First you cross an open triangle of ground, past a building on your right, before following the path through the allotments and between the housing estate. Cross Wye Bank Road and walk through the Rutland Recreation Ground, bearing right at the toilet block to gain Granby Road. Continue along Water Street to reach Rutland Square.

HADDON HALL—Building began in the 11th Century, and the present Hall was not completed until 400 years later. Today it is regarded as the finest manorial home in England. Much of the work was done by the Vernon family; Sir George Vernon made the Long Gallery in the mid-16th Century. His daughter married Sir John Manners, and the Manners (Rutlands) have owned the building ever since. Dorothy and Sir John eloped from the Hall and were married in Leicestershire. Their story is now one of Derbyshire's best-loved stories. Monuments to them can be seen in Bakewell Parish Church. In the early 1700s the Dukes of Rutland were busy building Belvoir Castle in Leicestershire and Haddon Hall was abandoned. Early this century a later Duke took interest in his ancestral home and restored it back to its former glory. The Hall makes a very interesting visit.

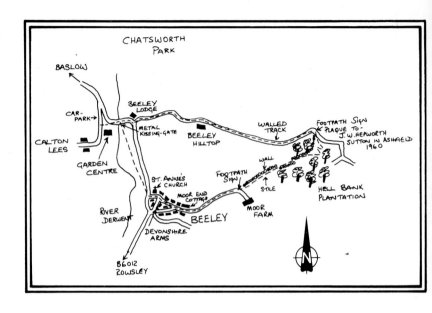

CHATSWORTH HOUSE AND GARDENS

BEELEY—wood and moor—
3 miles—*allow 1½hours*

MAPS—O.S. 1:25,000 Outdoor Leisure Map—The White Peak (East Sheet) - O.S. 1:50,000 Sheet No 119—Buxton, Matlock and Dovedale

CAR PARK—Chatsworth/Calton Lees road junction. G.R. SK259684.

ABOUT THE WALK—This walk, to the immediate south of Chatsworth Park, is full of historical interest whilst providing an ascent through woodland to moorland and extensive views.

WALKING INSTRUCTIONS—From the car park walk towards the Chatsworth Garden Centre, and turn left down the path to the road bridge over the River Derwent. On the other side, as foothpath—signposted, turn right through the metal kissing gate and follow the path across the field to Beeley Church. Cross the road and walk up past the Church on your left. Bear right, and left almost immediately, with a solitary tree and grass triangle on your right. The road on your right descends to the Devonshire Arms. Continue through Beeley, passing Norman House on your right and Moor End Cottage on your left. You are now on a 'No Through Road'. Where the lane, now a track, turns right across Beeley Brook to Moor Farm, keep straight ahead, as footpath—signposted, with the stone wall on your immediate left.

After the second field on your left, pass through a stile with the field boundary now on your right and the edge of Beeley Plantation. Shortly after a gate, the forest curves to your left. Here on your right you enter the forest—a water trough is a little ahead on your left in the open field. At first you have a wide path to follow, before crossing a brook and beginning a zig-zag ascent. The path from here becomes confusing because of the preponderance of side paths. After no more than ten minutes, you gain a wide track. Turn left along this to the head of a small valley. Here is a sharp bend in the road, footpath sign and plaque in memory of J.W. Hepworth, Sutton in Ashfield 1960. Turn left, and begin descending the rough walled track through a small plantation known as Rounds, and on to Beeley Hilltop. Here the track becomes tarmaced surface as you descend to Beeley Lodge and the road. Keep straight ahead and cross the bridge over the River Derwent and retrace your steps back to the car park.

BEELEY—St. Anne's Church—dates from 1150 A.D. with a Norman doorway. The tower is 14th Century, but much of the church was rebuilt in 1884. The interior contains several memorials to the Cavendish family.

The village contains several old houses, including an old Hall, which was formerly the Manor House but by the end of the 16th Century was a farmhouse. The Devonshire Arms is a former coaching inn.

BEELEY HILL TOP—early 16th Century house and part of the Chatsworth estate. In the middle of this century the building lay derelict, but has been very carefully restored. The interior contains Elizabethan fireplaces, oak panelling and Jacobean plasterwork.

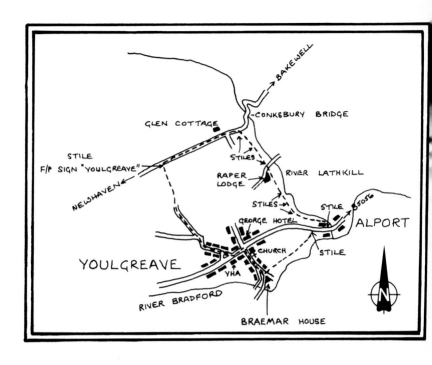

LATHKILL DALE

ALPORT—Lathkill Dale and Youlgreave—
3 miles—*allow 1 1/2 hours*

MAPS—O.S. 1:25,000 Series Outdoor Leisure Map—The White Peak (East Sheet) O.S. 1:50,000 Series—Sheet No. 119—Buxton, Matlock and Dovedale.

CAR PARK—Alport village.

ABOUT THE WALK—A delightful walk; first along a dale, before crossing fields to Youlgreave village and its imposing church; and finally a high-level walk above the River Bradford back to Alport.

WALKING INSTRUCTIONS—Cross the Youlgreave road (B5056) at Alport, to the Lathkill River, where you will find the path, stile and footpath sign. Follow the well-used path up the dale with the river on your right at first. After four fields you begin leaving the river to gain the track beside Raper Lodge. Cross the track and continue on the path to the Conksbury road ¼ mile away. Where the path dips to the right, bear left with the wall on your left to the stile and road. Turn left and ascend the road, passing Glen Cottage on your right. Continue ascending on the Newhaven road. At the top of the hill is the footpath sign—'Youlgreave'—and stile on your left. The path line is temporarily diverted because of mining, but is well—stiled and signposted as you head southwards. After ¼ mile you reach a walled grass track. Continue on this to the tarmaced road and footpath sign—'Over Haddon'. Turn left and descend the lane to Youlgreave, bearing left in the village to reach the main street opposite the Youth Hostel. Turn left, and opposite the George Hotel turn right down the lane, with the church on your immediate left. Keep left at the first road junction, and at the second turn left onto the path opposite Braemar House. The path maintains height with the limestone wall on your left. Below is the River Bradford. Follow the high level path to the B5056 road. Turn right and descend to Alport.

LATHKILL DALE—The river is one of the purest in England, and the water is exceptionally clear. Coots, moorhens and mallard ducks are often seen.

YOULGREAVE—The Youth Hostel was formerly the local Co-op. Dominating the village is All Saints Church; the 15th Century perpendicular tower is the finest in Derbyshire. Amongst the gravestones can be seen an upturned font. The font inside is unique and once belonged to nearby Elton, and incorporates a holy stoup. There are several monuments inside, including a 12th Century monument to Sir John Rossington; a tomb to Thomas Cokayne, who died in 1488; and an alabaster panel to Robert Gilbert and his family. The church is one of the few in Derbyshire to record having a dog-whipper. His duty was to 'whip the dogs out of the church before divine service'. In 1716 the dog-whipper was paid 7 pence a year for this service.

The unique Derbyshire well-dressing ceremony takes place in Youlgreave in June.

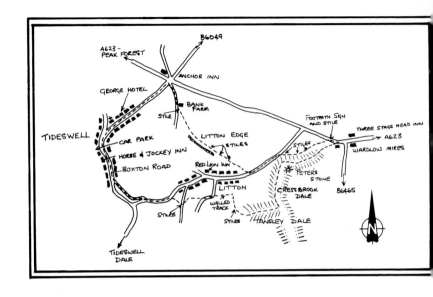

GEORGE HOTEL

TIDESWELL—Two Dales and Four Inns—
4½ miles—*allow 2½ hours*

MAPS—O.S. 1:25,000 Outdoor Leisure Map—The White Peak (East Sheet). O.S. 1:50,000 Series—Sheet No. 119—Buxton, Matlock and Dovedale.

CAR PARK—Central Tideswell—Cherry Tree Square.

ABOUT THE WALK—From Tideswell this walk takes you past the village of Litton before descending Tansley Dale to Cressbrook Dale. For your return to Tideswell you walk along Litton Edge before entering the village and passing the magnificent 14th Century church.

WALKING INSTRUCTIONS—From the car park turn right and walk along Buxton Road, passing the Horse and Jockey Inn on your right. ¼ mile later, opposite a bus shelter, turn left along a narrow lane signposted 'Unsuitable for Motors'. Follow this lane above the main road, and round to your left into Litton Dale and the road to Litton. Cross the road and walk up the righthand side along a tarmaced path. ¼ mile later and opposite Dale House turn right, as footpath-signposted, and ascend the field to a stile and road. Cross both, and bear left to the next stile before keeping straight ahead with the wall on your left and through the many stiles. Litton village is just below you with the Red Lion Inn. Continue ahead along a minor road, and where it bears left keep straight ahead on the walled farm track. At the fourth field on your right, as footpath—signposted, turn right and descend the field before bearing left and descending Tansley Dale. At the junction with Cressbrook Dale where there is a National Nature Reserve sign, turn left and follow the path along the dale floor and past the limestone knoll—Peter's Stone on your right. Continue along the path to the road junction at Wardlow Mires, reached via a stile on the right of a farm building. Just ahead of you is the Three Stags Inn.

Turn left along the A623 road, and 150 yards later turn left onto the signposted path which climbs above Cressbrook Dale. First you keep the wall on your immediate right to a stile, before crossing the subsequent field to the top left-hand corner and stile. Keep the next wall on your right and ascend to the Litton road, gained via a stile. Turn left and ascend the road ¼ mile. At the top, just past a drive on your left, turn right onto a track and gain a stile ahead. The next field has a gap on the right before reaching a stile in the top left of the field above Litton Edge. The next ¼ mile is well-stiled, and should be easy to follow as you hug the edge before bearing right to the stile and road at Bank Farm. Turn right along the road to the crossroads at Anchor Inn. Turn left and walk down the road into Tideswell, passing the George Hotel on your right and the church. The car park is reached by walking along Church Street on your left.

TIDESWELL—contains many buildings of the 18th Century, but is dominated by the church, the most complete 14th Century church in England. Inside is a wealth of features, including a 14th Century font, oak carvings, and several brasses.

INNS—Anchor Inn—more than 500 years old. Was a farm house before becoming a coaching inn.

George Hotel—built in 1730, and has venetian windows and oak-panelled rooms. Former coaching inn.

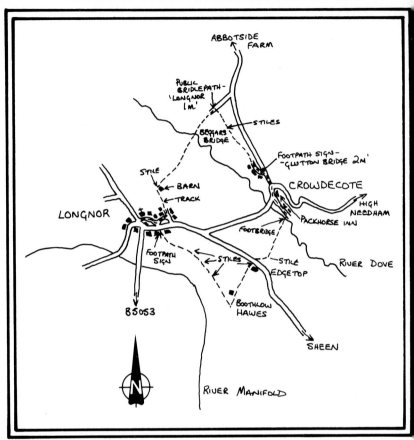

PACKHORSE INN —CROWDECOTE

LONGNOR—Dove and Manifold Valley—
3 miles—*allow 1½ hours*

MAPS—O.S. 1:25,000 Outdoor Leisure Map—The White Peak (West Sheet). O.S. 1:50,000 Series—Sheet No. 119—Buxton, Matlock and Dovedale.

CAR PARK—Longnor Market Place.

ABOUT THE WALK—A short walk, first above the infant Manifold River before crossing the ridge to the River Dove and Derbyshire and an inn at Crowdecote. A short walk along the valley floor returns you to the Dove and an ascent back to Longnor.

WALKING INSTRUCTIONS—From the Market Place turn left along the Crowdecote road. Just past the Cheshire Cheese Inn, turn right down a farm track; footpath-signposted. In the farmyard turn left to the stile. Cross the next field to the stile before bearing left, and begin crossing ten narrow strip fields. The stiles are readily seen, making route-finding no problem. After the tenth field, walk in front of Crofts Farm, bearing right following the stiles. In less than ¼ mile you reach a ruined barn. Here turn left over a stile, with the stone wall on your right as you cross the field to the right-hand side of Boothlaw Hawes. Pass through the gate and continue ascending up the field to the left-hand side of Edgetop. Here you reach a minor road from Longnor. Turn right and left almost immediately over a stile. Bear right and descend steeply at first to a stile. Keep straight ahead, descending the field to a footbridge over the River Dove. Ascend to the track, where you turn left for Crowdecote village and the Packhorse Inn.

Just past the inn turn left on the minor road, and shortly afterwards turn left onto a track, as footpath-signposted —'Glutton Bridge 2 miles'. First you pass several buildings on your left before continuing across the fields, keeping the field boundary on your right. After the fourth field you cross the open field to a stile, and after the next field reach the 'Bridlepath to Longnor'. Here turn left along the walled track to the River Dove and footbridge known as Beggar's Bridge. Ascend the field beyond, passing a small water trough just over the brow on your left. Continue ahead, aiming for the right of a farm building. Turn left here and ascend the track up the valley side above the sewage works. At the top you re-enter Longnor. Walk past the houses, and turn right down the lane with the council houses on your left and Mount Pleasant on your right. At the bottom turn right and follow the road to the church. Here at the entrance gate turn left along Chapel Street back to the Market Place.

LONGNOR—A fascinating village well worth exploring. Above the Market Place is a toll board. In 1903 the toll for 'every basket of eggs or other articles for sale... One Penny'.

The classical-style church was built in 1780, and the outside appears to be two-storey, but inside there is a false ceiling. Amongst the gravestones can be seen one to William Billings, who died on January 25th 1791, aged 112.

CROWDECOTE—Former packhorse route across the River Dove, as the inn's name suggests. The name of the village stems from 'Crawdy Coat Bridge', which was originally wooden. A stone packhorse bridge was built here in 1709.

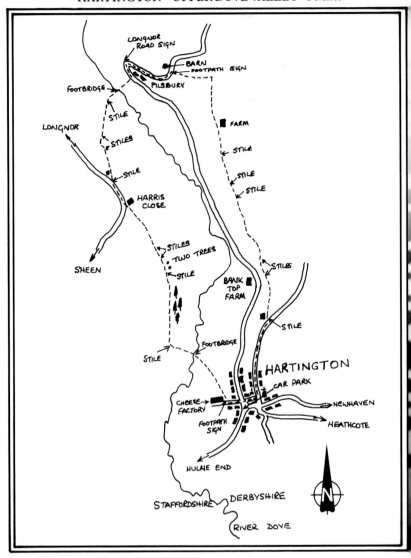

HARTINGTON—St. Giles Church dates from the 14th Century. Inside the main door can be seen a memorial to Thomas Mellor, who died on 6th December 1822, aged 103. The south transept contains a unique set of panels of the Patriarchs of Israel and date from about 1700.

CHEESE FACTORY—Derbyshire was once a principal cheese—producing county, and had in 1870 at Longford the first cheese factory in England. Today the cheese factory at Hartington is the only one left producing stilton and green sage cheese.

CHARLES COTTON—The River Dove is always associated with two of England's immortal fishermen, Charles Cotton and Isaac Walton. Cotton's fishing house lies on private ground ¾ mile south of Hartington. A hotel is named after Charles Cotton just off the square, and Isaac Walton wrote the famous book, The Compleat Angler.

HARTINGTON—Upper Dove Valley—
5 miles—*allow 2½ hours*

MAPS—O.S. 1:25,000 Outdoor Leisure Map—The White Peak (West Sheet). O.S. 1:50,000 Series—Sheet No. 119—Buxton, Matlock and Dovedale.

CAR PARK—Hartington Square.

ABOUT THE WALK—Hartington, close to the Staffordshire boundary, is a popular walking centre for the limestone dales of Beresford, Wolfscote and Biggin. To the immediate north of Hartington is a more open valley, through which the River Dove flows. This high level circuit of the Dove valley passes through delightful quiet countryside away from the crowds.

WALKING INSTRUCTIONS—From the square turn left (due west) along the 'No Through Road', past 'Stoney Well' to the entrance of Hartington's cheese factory— J.M. Nuttall & Co. Turn right as footpath-signposted, and walk through the factory's righthand side to a stile and footpath sign. Continue diagonally left across the field, on a defined path to further stiles. Bearing slightly left, you reach the infant River Dove and footbridge. Cross this and step into Staffordshire. Continue up the field to a stile on the left of a gate. Here turn right and begin ascending on a wide grass track to a pine plantation. The stile here admits you into the edge of the plantation. Keep the gritstone wall on your left as you cross a field beyond the trees. The next field is open; simply keep to the left of two solitary trees to reach the next stile. Keep the wall on your left side, and four fields bring you to the Sheen road beside Harris Close, built in 1842.

Turn right along the road, and after 200 yards on your right is a gate and stile on its righthand side. Pass through this and walk past farm buildings on your left to a stile. You now begin descending almost due northwards down the valley side. The path ahead is well indicated by the stiles. After the third stile you enter a large field. Simply aim for the pine trees, where there is a stile onto a walled track. Turn right and cross a footbridge over the River Dove and return to Derbyshire. The walls on the Staffordshire side of the Dove are gritstone, but on the Derbyshire side they are limestone. Continue up the track to the minor road of Pilsbury. Turn left and follow the road round to your right above the farm, signposted for Longnor.

Above the farm the road turns sharp left, and a few yards later you approach a solitary barn on your left. Just before it turn right, as signposted, and cross the field, passing a solitary stone and dew pond. At the end of the field, instead of ascending the stile, turn right and ascend to the field corner. Cross the wall and skirt the walls on your left as you descend to a farm on your left. Cross the field in front of the farm to a stile and on to the next. This last section is the only awkward bit on the walk, as it is not well-stiled and there is no distinct path to follow. However, two fields from the farm the path and stiles get better. First maintain height as you cross the next curving field to a stile. For the next three fields you keep just above the final slope of the valley as you aim for the farm track above Bank Top Farm, ½ mile away. Walk up the track a few yards before bearing right with the wall on your right. Ascend a stile and continue across two final fields to the left of a large modern barn and gain a minor road. Turn right and follow this road down into Hartington a little over ¼ mile away. Turn right at the church and descend to the Square.

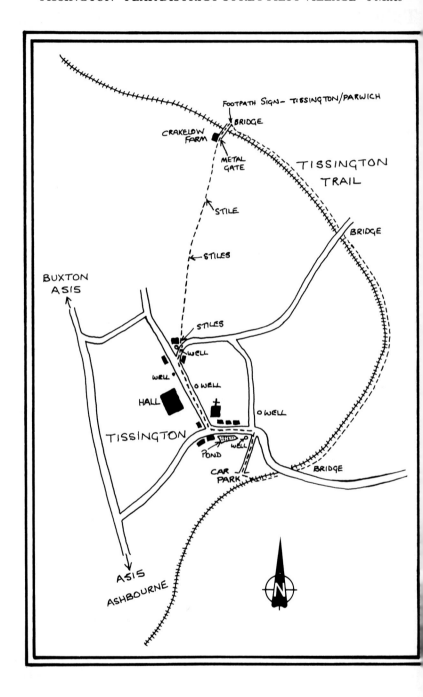

TISSINGTON—a look at the Peak District's prettiest village—3 miles—*allow 1½ hours*

MAPS—O.S. 1:25,000 Outdoor Leisure Map—The White Peak (West Sheet). O.S. 1:50,000 Series—Sheet No. 119—Buxton, Matlock and Dovedale.

CAR PARK—Southern end of village beside Tissington Trail.

ABOUT THE WALK—Sheltered from main roads, Tissington has retained its splendid past with ancient customs, impressive Hall and centuries' old church. This short walk takes you down the main street past its buildings and along the line of an old railway line—The Tissington Trail.

WALKING INSTRUCTIONS—From the car park turn left and walk along the trail for the next 1½ miles. On approaching the third overhead bridge turn right, as signposted—Tissington and Parwich—and leave the trail. Cross the bridge to your left, and pass through Crakelow Farm before bearing left and heading almost due south to Tissington. The pathline is not always noticeable on the ground, but all the time you can see the stiles ahead, guiding you. At the village road turn right, then left down the main road past the Hall on your right, and the church on your left. At the bottom bear left, passing the village pond on your right. Shortly afterwards turn right down the car park entrance.

TISSINGTON—

HALL—The Fitzherbert family have lived here for 400 years. The present hall was started in 1609 by Francis Fitzherbert. The wrought iron gates were made by Robert Bakewell in about 1720. The Hall's gardens are open to the public on two Saturday afternoons, under the National Gardens Scheme.

CHURCH—dedicated to St. Mary and dates from Norman times. Above the entrance porch is a Norman Tympanum. Inside is an 11th Century font, several monuments to the Fitzherbert family, 16th Century communion rails and several extremely beautiful stained glass windows.

WELL DRESSING—a unique Derbyshire custom dating back to 1350. Tissington has five wells, and during the Black Death—1348/9—many people died but the Tissington wells contained pure water and everyone who drank from them survived. As an offering of thanks the wells have been 'dressed' ever since annually. Several other Derbyshire villages dress their wells, but Tissington's are the first on Ascension Day in May. The colourful mosaics of flowers portray a biblical or topical scene.

TISSINGTON HALL

27

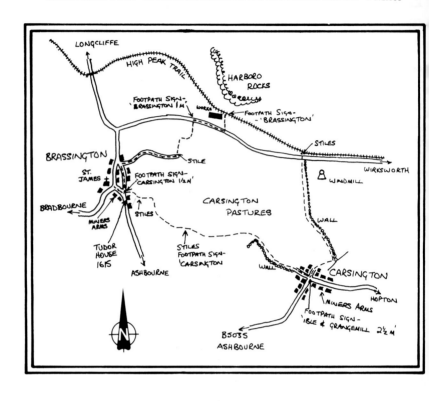

HARBORO ROCKS

BRASSINGTON—Dolomitic limestone and High Peak Trail—5 miles—*allow 2½ hours*

MAPS—O.S. 1:25,000 Outdoor Leisure Map—The White Peak (East Sheet). O.S. 1:50,000 Series Sheet No. 119—Buxton, Matlock and Dove Dale.

CAR PARK—No official car park.

ABOUT THE WALK—You explore the high limestone plateau and two limestone villages, before passing a section of dolomitic limestone and walking along a section of the High Peak Trail.

WALKING INSTRUCTIONS—Start the walk from the road junction beneath St. James' Church in Brassington, and descend the road past the Miner's Arms. At the bottom turn left; opposite and to your right is an imposing building, known as Tudor House and built in 1615. Almost immediately turn right and follow the signposted path—Carsington 1½ miles. Descend a stile and steps before reaching open fields. Bear right across two fields, ascending gently. Once through the second stile turn left and ascend with the wall on your left. At the top turn right, keeping the wall on your right. After the next stile, the path crosses an abandoned lead mining area before reaching a walled track. Cross this as signposted—'Carsington'. Ascend the next field before bearing slightly left to the field corner. Keep to the lefthand track as you curve round to the right to a wall on your immediate right. Begin descending onto a lane and into Carsington. In the village is another Miner's Arms.

Upon meeting the B5035 road, turn left and ascend between the houses, as footpath-signposted—'Ible and Grangemill 2½ miles'. Bear right at the top house, which has a plaque to Private A.R. Pike, who was lost on Pilgrim Ridge in Belgium on July 31st, 1917. Ascend the slope to your right to the wood. At the top don't cross the stile, but turn left and keep the wall on your immediate right as you follow it around the eastern side of Carsington Pastures for the next ¾ mile. In the field on your right can be seen the tower of Carsington windmill. Cross the road via the stiles and reach the High Peak Trail. Turn left and walk along this for the next ½ mile. On your right is Harborough Rocks. As you approach the factory, leave the trail, as signposted 'Footpath—Brassington', and walk along the track to the road. Turn right and ¼ mile later turn left, as signposted 'Brassington'. Keep the wall on your left as you follow it straight ahead, then right, before descending to the end of a tarmaced road. Turn right and descend the lane to the northern end of Brassington. Turn left at the road and shortly afterwards turn right, back into central Brassington and St. James' Church.

BRASSINGTON—Limestone village, whose church contains Norman remains. In the area are several outcrops of dolomitic limestone—Rainster and Harborough Rocks—the only place in Derbyshire where this rock is found. Although no more than 30 feet high, they are a popular climbing ground.

HIGH PEAK TRAIL—Formerly a railway that linked the Peak Forest Canal at Whaley Bridge with the Cromford Canal at Cromford. Was built in the 1830's at a cost of £180,000. Converted to a pedestrian way in 1972.

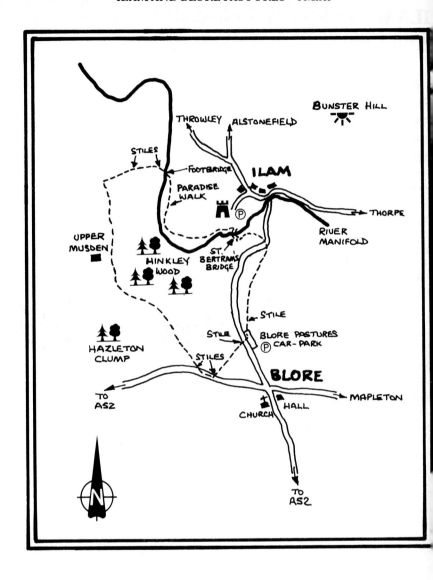

RIVER MANIFOLD—on Paradise Walk can be seen the bubble holes where the River Manifold re-emerges. The river disappears down a swallet near Wettonmill five miles to the north. The Battle Stone was found in a house wall in Ilam last century and is believed to be Saxon.

BLORE—

CHURCH—small unusual church with box pews and two-decker pulpit. The chapel houses a huge tomb to the Basset family and was made about 1640.

ILAM and Blore Pastures—
4 miles—*allow 1½hours*

MAPS—1:25,000 Series Outdoor Leisure Map—The White Peak (West Sheet). 1:25,000 Sheet No SK 04/14—Ashbourne and the Churnet Valley 1:50,000 Series Sheet No. 119—Buxton, Matlock and Dovedale.

CAR PARK—Blore Pastures, car park and picnic area. Near Blore on Ilam-Blore road.

ABOUT THE WALK—Ilam and the Manifold Valley are two of the scenic gems of the Staffordshire side of the Peak District. This short walk takes you to both, and provides a magnificent viewpoint across to Thorpe Cloud and Dovedale. On return to the car park you have the option to visit a fascinating church.

WALKING INSTRUCTIONS—Leave the car park by the southern end (Ilam) where there is a stile. Begin descending to another stile before crossing an open field to the unfenced Ilam-Blore road. Cross the road onto a grass track and follow this curving track to your left as you descend and enter the National Trust Ilam estate. Pass a building on your left and descend the rough track to the River Manifold and St. Bertram's Bridge, that was restored in 1839. Cross the bridge and turn left, and follow the well-used path around the estate, first beside the River Manifold and then along Paradise Walk and past the Battle Stone on your right. In Ilam Hall the National Trust have an information office, and there is a tea room.

At the end of Paradise Walk you reach a footbridge on your left. Cross this and the field beyond, bearing to your right to the stile. Now the hard work begins, as you ascend directly up the field to another stile. The next field has little evidence of a path, but simply continue uphill, passing the remains of a wall on your right. At the top you reach a farm track, where you turn left. The effort to get here is well worth it, for the views are exceptional. Follow the track to a gate with a water trough on your left. Continue on, keeping the stone wall on your righthand side. The true right of way goes to the ruins of Upper Musden Farm before returning to the valley side, but the stiles are not there. It is better to keep the wall on your right before crossing an open field and descending a shallow valley to a gate and noticeable track, the true right of way. Ascend the other side as you curve around the hillside, with Hazleton Clump on your right and Hinkley Wood beneath you. The path line bears right as you cross the fields away from the Manifold Valley. The stiles guide you, and in ¼ mile you reach the minor road and stile. Turn left along the road, and 150 yards later turn left over the stile and cross the field, bringing you to another stile directly opposite the car park. Instead of crossing this field you can continue along the road to Blore and visit its church, then return to the car park via the Ilam road.

ILAM—

CHURCH—dedicated to the Holy Cross. Inside it has a Saxon font; a tomb to St. Bertram and two funeral garlands, a relic of an 18th Century custom. The Chantry Chapel has a carving by Sir Francis Chantry of Sir David Pike-Watts.

HALL—built by the Watts-Russell family in the 19th Century, and was given to the National Trust in 1934. Part of the building is now a Youth Hostel, and is reputedly haunted by a white lady.

EQUIPMENT NOTES
—some personal thoughts

BOOTS—perferably with a leather upper, of medium weight, with a vibram sole I always add a foam cushioned insole to help cushion the base of my feet.

SOCKS—I generally wear two thick pairs as this helps to minimise blisters. The inner pair of loop stitch variety and approximately 80% wool. The outer a thick rib pair of approximately 80% wool.

WATERPROOFS—for general walking I wear a T shirt or shirt with a cotton wind jacket on top. You generate heat as you walk and I prefer to layer my clothes to avoid getting too hot. Depending on the season will dictate how many layers you wear. In soft rain I just use my wind jacket for I know it quickly dries out. In heavy downpours I slip on a neoprene lined cagoule, and although hot and clammy it does keep me reasonably dry. Only in extreme conditions will I don overtrousers, much preferring to get wet and feel comfortable.

FOOD—as I walk I carry bars of chocolate, for they provide instant energy and are light to carry. In winter a flask of hot coffee is welcome. I never carry water and find no hardship from doing so, but this is a personal matter. From experience I find the more I drink the more I want. You should always carry some extra food such as Kendal Mint Cake for emergencies.

RUCKSACK—for day walking I use a climbing rucksac of about 40 litre capacity and although excess space it does mean that the sac is well padded and with a shoulder strap. Inside apart from the basics for the day I carry gloves, balaclava, spare pullover and a pair of socks.

MAP & COMPASS—when I am walking I always have the relevant map—usually 1:25,000 scale—open in my hand. This enables me to constantly check that I am walking the right way. In case of bad weather I carry a Silva type compass, which once mastered gives you complete confidence in thick cloud or mist.

ILAM CHURCH

OTHER BOOKS BY JOHN N. MERRILL & PUBLISHED BY JNM PUBLICATIONS

DAY WALK GUIDES

PEAK DISTRICT: SHORT CIRCULAR WALKS Fifteen carefully selected walks—3 to 5 miles—starting from a car park. The walks cover the variety of the area—the gritstone edges, limestone dales, and peat moorland. All follow well defined paths; include a pub for lunch; and are suitable for all the family. 44 pages 16 maps 32 photographs   ISBN 0 907496 16 4

PEAK DISTRICT TOWN WALKS Twelve short circular walks around the principal towns and villages of the Peak District. Including Castleton, Buxton, Hathersage, Eyam, Tissington and Ashbourne. Each walk has a detailed map and extensive historical notes complete with pictures. 60 pages 12 maps 96 photographs   ISBN 0 907496 20 2

PEAK DISTRICT: LONG CIRCULAR WALKS Fifteen differing walks 12 to 18 miles long for the serious hiker. Many follow lesser used paths in the popular areas, giving a different perspective to familiar landmarks. 64 pages 16 maps 28 photographs   ISBN 0 907496 17 2

WESTERN PEAKLAND—CIRCULAR WALKS The first book to cover this remarkably attractive side of the National Park—west of Buxton. The guide combines both long and short walks. 25 -3 to 11 mile long walks with extremely detailed maps to help you explore the area. 48 pages 23 maps 22 photographs   ISBN 0 907496 15 6

12 SHORT CIRCULAR WALKS AROUND MATLOCK 12 walks of about 4 miles long into the Matlock area rich in history and folklore and make ideal family outings. Included is an 'alpine' walk, using Matlock Bath's cable car as part of the route. 52 pages 44 photographs 12 maps   ISBN 0 907496 25 3

SHORT CIRCULAR WALKS IN THE DUKERIES More than 25 walks in the Nottinghamshire/Sherwood Forest area, past many of the historic buildings that make up the Dukeries area.   ISBN 0 907496 29 6

DERBYSHIRE AND THE PEAK DISTRICT CANAL WALKS More than 20 walks both short and long along the canals in the area—Cromford, Erewash, Chesterfield, Derby, Trent, Peak Forest and Macclesfield canals.
ISBN 0 907496 30 X

HIKE TO BE FIT: STROLLING WITH JOHN John Merrill's personal guide to walking in the countryside to keep fit and healthy. He describes what equipment to use, where to go, how to map read, use a compass and what to do about blisters! 36 pages 23 photos 2 sketches 3 charts   ISBN 0 907496 19 9

CHALLENGE WALKS

JOHN MERRILL'S PEAK DISTRICT CHALLENGE WALK A 25 mile circular walk from Bakewell, across valleys and heights involving 3,700 feet of ascent. More than 2,000 people have already completed the walk. A badge and completion certificate is available to those who complete. 32 pages 18 photographs 9 maps
ISBN 0 907496 18 0

JOHN MERRILL'S YORKSHIRE DALES CHALLENGE WALK A 23 mile circular walk from Kettlewell in the heart of the Dales. The route combines mountain, moorlands, limestone country and dale walking with 3,600 feet of ascent. A badge and certificate is available to those who complete the route. 3° pages 16 photographs 8 maps
ISBN 0 907196 28 8

THE RIVER'S WAY A two day walk of 43 miles, down the length of the Peak District National Park. Inaugurated and created by John, the walk starts at Edale the end of the Pennine Way, and ends at Ilam. Numerous hostels campgrounds, B&B, and pubs lie on the route, as you follow the five main river systems of the Peak—Noe, Derwent, Wye, Dove, and Manifold. 52 pages 3° photographs 7 maps
ISBN 0 907496 08 3

PEAK DISTRICT: HIGH LEVEL ROUTE A hard 90 mile, weeks walk, around the Peak District, starting from Matlock. As the title implies the walk keeps to high ground while illustrating the dramatic landscape of the Peak District.The walk was inaugurated and created by John and is used by him for training for his major walks! 60 pages 31 photographs 13 maps
ISBN 0 907496 10 5

PEAK DISTRICT MARATHONS The first reference book to gather together all the major and classical long walks of the Peak District between 25 and 50 miles long. Many are challenge walks with badges and completion cards for those who complete. The longest walk—280 miles —inaugurated by John is around the entire Derbyshire boundary. Each walk has a general map, accommodation list, and details of what guides and maps are needed. 56 pages 20 photographs 20 maps
ISBN 0 907496 13 X

HISTORICAL GUIDES

WINSTER—A VISITOR'S GUIDE A detailed look at a former lead mining community which still retains a Morris dancing team and annual pancake races. A two mile walk brings you to many historical buildings including the 17th century Market House. Illustrated by old photographs. 20 pages 21 photographs 1 map
ISBN 0 907496 21 0

DERBYSHIRE INNS The first book to tell the story behind more than 150 inns in the Peak District and Derbyshire area. With details of legends, murders and historical anecdotes, the book gives added pleasure or impetus to explore the pubs of the region. Profusely illustrated with 65 photographs and a brief history of brewing in Derbyshire. 68 pages 57 photographs 5 maps ISBN 0 907496 11 3

100 HALLS AND CASTLES OF THE PEAK DISTRICT AND DERBYSHIRE
A visitor's guide to the principal historical buildings of the region. Many are open to the public and the guide describes the history of the building from the Domesday Book to the present time.The book is illustrated by 120 photographs and makes an excellent souvenir gift of one of England's finest architectural areas. 120 pages 116 photographs 4 maps
ISBN 0 907496 23 7

TOURING THE PEAK DISTRICT AND DERBYSHIRE Twenty circular routes of about 50 miles for the motorist or cyclist. Each route has a set theme, such as the gritstone edges or in the steps of Mary, Queen of Scots. Deatiled maps for each route and fifty photographs make this a useful companion to the Peak District/Derbyshire area. 76 pages 45 photographs 20 maps
ISBN 0 907496 22 9

JOHN'S MARATHON WALKS

EMERALD COAST WALK The story of John's walk up the total length of the west coast of Ireland and exploration of more than fifty islands—1,600 miles. 132 pages 32 photographs 12 maps
ISBN 0 907496 02 4

TURN RIGHT AT LAND'S END In 1978 John Merrill became the first person to walk the entire coastline of Britain—6,824 miles in ten months. The book details the route, how he ascended our three major mountains and how he found a wife. Included are more than 200 photographs he took on the walk, which is also a unique guide to our coastline. 246 pages 214 photographs 10 maps
ISBN 0 907496 24 5

WITH MUSTARD ON MY BACK John has gathered together the stories of his first decade of walking—1970-1980. Here is a collection of unique walks in Britain, from a 2,000 mile walk linking the ten National Parks of England and Wales together to a 450 mile walk from Norwich to Durham.
ISBN 0 907496 27 X

TURN RIGHT AT DEATH VALLEY During the summer of 1984, John walked coast to coast across America, a distance of 4,226 miles in 177 days. Few have walked across and none have taken so difficult a route. He crossed all the main mountain ranges, climbed 14,000 foot mountains, crossed deserts in 100 degrees, walked rim to rim of the Grand Canyon in 8½ hours, and crossed the famed Death Valley. The walk is without parallel and the story is the remarkable tale of this unique adventure.
ISBN 0 907496 26 1

THE RAMBLER INN—EDALE

WALK RECORD CHART

Date Walked

INTRODUCTION ....
EDALE—RUSHUP EDGE—6 Miles ....
HOPE—WIN HILL—4 Miles ....
STANAGE EDGE—ALONG A GRITSTONE EDGE—3 Miles ....
HATHERSAGE—A HISTORICAL WALK 4 Miles ....
BASLOW—EDGES WALK—5 Miles ....
BAKEWELL TOWN WALK—1½ Miles ....
BAKEWELL—WYE VALLEY AND HADDON HALL—4 Miles ....
BEELEY—WOOD AND MOOR—3 Miles ....
ALPORT—LATHKILL DALE AND YOULGREAVE—3 Miles ....
TIDESWELL—TWO DALES AND FOUR INNS—4½ Miles ....
LONGNOR—DOVE AND MANIFOLD VALLEY—3 Miles ....
HARTINGTON—UPPER DOVE VALLEY—5 Miles ....
TISSINGTON—PEAK DISTRICT'S PRETTIEST VILLAGE—3 Miles ....
BRASSINGTON—LIMESTONE AND HIGH PEAK TRAIL—5 Miles ....
ILAM AND BLORE PASTURES—4 Miles ....

GET A JOHN MERRILL WALKING BADGE—complete six of these walks and send details and £1.50 payable to JNM Publications.

WALKING IN CHATSWORTH

36